Change the World for Ten Bucks

Cataloging in Publication Data:
A catalog record for this publication is available from the National Library of Canada.

First printing August 2006.

Cover design by Whybins/TBWA Australia adapted for Canada by Diane McIntosh.

First published in Great Britain 2004 as **Change the World for a Fiver** by Short Books Ltd.

Printed in Canada by Friesens.
Third printing November 2007.

New Society Publishers acknowledges the support of the Government of Canada through the Book Publishing Industry Development Program (BPIDP) for our publishing activities.

Paperback ISBN 13: 978-1-55092-300-1
Paperback ISBN 10: 1-55092-300-5

Inquiries regarding requests to reprint all or part of **Change the World for Ten Bucks** should be addressed to New Society Publishers at the address below.

To order directly from the publishers, please call toll-free (North America) 1-800-567-6772, or order online at www.newsociety.com

Any other inquiries can be directed by mail to:

New Society Publishers P.O. Box 189, Gabriola Island, BC V0R 1X0, Canada
1-800-567-6772

New Society Publishers' mission is to publish books that contribute in fundamental ways to building an ecologically sustainable and just society, and to do so with the least possible impact on the environment, in a manner that models this vision. We are committed to doing this not just through education, but through action. We are acting on our commitment to the world's remaining ancient forests by phasing out our paper supply from ancient forests worldwide. This book is one step toward ending global deforestation and climate change. It is printed on acid-free paper that is 100% old growth forest-free (100% post-consumer recycled), processed chlorine free, and printed with vegetable-based, low-VOC inks. For further information, or to browse our full list of books and purchase securely, visit our website at: www.newsociety.com

NEW SOCIETY PUBLISHERS   www.newsociety.com

Change the World for Ten Bucks

50 actions to change the world and make you feel good

Designed in the UK by Antidote
Creative team: Tim Ashton, Steve Henry, Ken Hoggins, Chris O'Shea,
Chris Wigan, David Robinson, Eugénie Harvey, Nick Walker and Paul Twivy.

Designed in Canada by N'lyven
Creative team: Noah Lieberman, Paul Edney
The development of Change The World For Ten Bucks
and We Are What We Do in Canada is led by Paul Edney.

n lyven
DESIGN

NEW SOCIETY PUBLISHERS

"If you think you're too small to make a difference, try sleeping in a room with a mosquito."

- African Proverb

We Are What We Do

We live in peculiar times. More communications devices than ever before connect us, yet more people live alone. We want to belong to communities but our cities can be very lonely places.

We buy things – more and more things – with more and more money; but they don't make us happy. Life satisfaction was higher during post-war rationing in the 1940s.

The rich are getting richer, but nearly 10% of Canadians are shockingly poor. The other 90% experience other kinds of poverty: most of us feel that our lives are missing something.

Membership in political parties and unions continues to decline, yet tens of thousands of Canadians took to the streets to protest the war on Iraq, and Canadians raised millions of dollars for Tsunami relief.

We feel things very deeply and we want to do something, but sometimes the scale of the issues make it difficult for us – how can I make a difference? What can I do? Nothing I do will make a difference anyway …

Surely, the question now is not what we can do alone but what we can achieve together.

It was Mahatma Gandhi who said "We must be the change we want to see in the world". In other words, we are what we do.

We Are What We Do is not a charity. We are not an institution, we are a new kind of movement – a movement with attitude. We are not trying to raise money, we are trying to raise awareness. We are trying to show that a simple shift in attitudes and day-to-day behavior has the power to change the world.

We invite you to be part of a new kind of global community; not of joiners but of independent doers following the same banner and answering the questions that we all want answered.

Who are we? We Are What We Do.

How to use this book

This is a book of simple, everyday actions we reckon pretty much all of us can do. If you're reading this book, chances are you, or someone you know, has actually done one of the actions already (Action 25 Recycle Your Books or Action 47 Buy a Copy of This Book for a Friend) so you're already on your way!

Each page has an action strip down the right-hand side. This says what the action is.

A number of pages feature references to organizations which can help you perform the actions – for example, Action 26 Give Blood features the website address for the Canadian Blood Services so you can find your nearest donation centre.

We've included a whole host of related websites in Action 49 Learn More, Do More, at the end of the book which will give you more information about the action and how to do it.

We're not suggesting that either the list of actions or of websites in Action 49 are definitive – but they are a start. And by the way, We Are What We Do does not receive any money for websites mentioned in this book.

We'd love to hear from you, either with suggestions for new actions, or suggestions for other helpful organizations and websites.

Please email us at suggestions@wearewhatwedo.ca

Give someone a kiss they'll remember for the rest of their life

Take five minutes to learn how to do the kiss of life. Better still, take a couple of days and do a first aid course (check out St. John Ambulance Canada www.sja.ca).

Let's face it, saving someone's life is cool. In fact, it's about as cool as you can possibly get.

And, if you do learn this skill, you might like to know that the person you help is statistically unlikely to be a stranger.

They're much more likely to be a friend or relative.

Imagine saving your best friend's life.

1. Call for help. Ask someone to call 911. Look, listen and feel for signs of breathing.

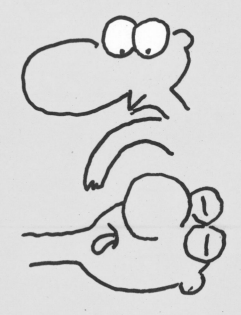

Illustration: Bruce Baldwin

2. If not breathing and there is no chance of neck injury, tilt head back, pinch nose and breathe into mouth.

3. Watch for a rise in chest, repeat breath and look for obvious signs of life. Continue breaths, once every four seconds, until help arrives or the person is breathing.

Call 911 for an ambulance

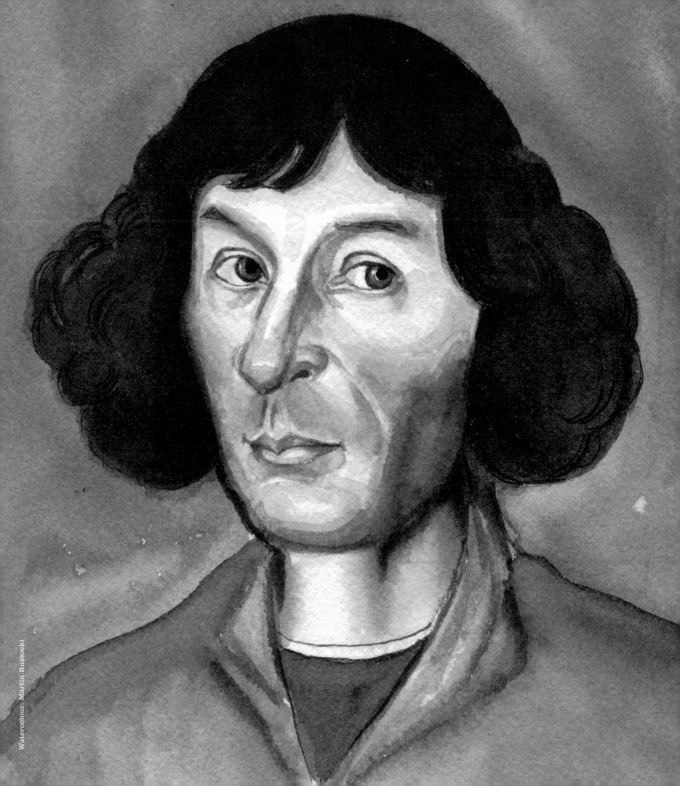

500 years is a long time

500 years ago, they thought the sun revolved around the earth (Until Nicolaus Copernicus, the dude on your left, put them right in 1514).

500 years ago, Magellan circumnavigated the globe.

500 years ago, Da Vinci painted the Mona Lisa.

Now imagine... 500 years from now, the 8 **billion** plastic bags we use this year in Canada will still be here.

There is an alternative.

It's called a canvas shopping bag and all major supermarkets now sell them for a few bucks.

Not only will using one help the planet but your oranges are less likely to burst through the bottom and roll down the street.

Read, tell a story, dance, sing, play with blocks, draw, do a puzzle. When kids ask you to play, it's because they know something you don't. They know you'll both feel richer for the experience.

A bus carries the same number of people as 50 cars. And it's going there anyway.

A friend of mine has
never forgotten seeing
his father kiss his
grandpa's hand as
he lay in a coma,
just before he died.

It was the only time
he had ever seen
them kiss.

And the only time he
hugged his father was
when his sister died.

It wasn't that they
weren't close, just that
they were grown up,
they were men, and only
death could take down all
the barriers.

But children do it
instinctively – they want
to touch and be touched,
to hold and be held.

So if there was one bit
of advice we'd give
everyone reading this
book, it would be this.

Touch someone you love.

Hold them.

Stroke them.

Kiss them.

It's the one piece of
magic we can all do,
every day.

Breathe

Plants are amazing things. They take in stuff we don't like (carbon dioxide) and pump out stuff we do (oxygen).

But we get rid of these amazing things by the millions every year.

In fact, 33 football fields of trees are cut down every minute worldwide.

Planting a tree or a native bush will not only help redress the balance, it'll also encourage native wildlife back to the area. Not to mention that each tree will provide oxygen for 2 people for the rest of their lives.

Which leads nicely to Action 6a – hug a tree.

Just let go before you get arrested.

Change a light bulb and see what you can save

An energy-saving light bulb might not seem cheap but over its lifetime it could save you $130 bucks and a lot more besides. Like the planet for example.

Illustration: Steve Heynen

Walk more

Obesity is turning into a massive problem in the developed world. One suggestion from doctors is to do something simple such as walking up a couple of flights of stairs every day.

Although that might seem a little pointless. Unless of course you were going there anyway.

So much for doctors.

But try walking as much as you can.

If that's only from the cake trolley to the cheese board and back again – well, that's a starter.

Well, no it isn't – it's a dessert. But you get the idea.

Happiness is a fairly traded banana

Fair-trade products guarantee to give the people who grow them a fair share of the profits. You'll see all sorts of fair-trade products in the shops these days – from bananas to coffee. So, if you buy a fair-trade banana, you can be proud of your banana.

And there are few feelings in this world that are better than being proud of your banana.

Spot the difference

If you turn your thermostat down by
one degree, you can save on average
$50 a year.

That's $4 a month you can put into
charity tins (see action 16).

It takes half as many muscles to smile as it does to frown.

And it makes you and others feel twice as good.

$$50 = 40 \times 2$$

At 50km/h, you are twice as likely to kill someone you hit as at 40km/h.

"Hello?? HELLO?? Can you hear me??"

There are 9.3 million mobile phones replaced in Canada every year.

That's a heck of a lot of annoying ringtones, and worse, it equates to around 1,000 tonnes of landfill (and a whole bunch of nasty chemicals).

So the next time you hear Beethoven's Fifth ring out at the movie theatre, resist the strong desire you have to grab the guy's phone and chuck it in the nearest garbage.

Pitch-in instead – go to www.pitch-in.ca to find a collection centre local to you.

TALK TO OLD PEOPLE
THEY KNOW
COOL STUFF
YOU DON'T
Photo: Tim Ashton / Antidote

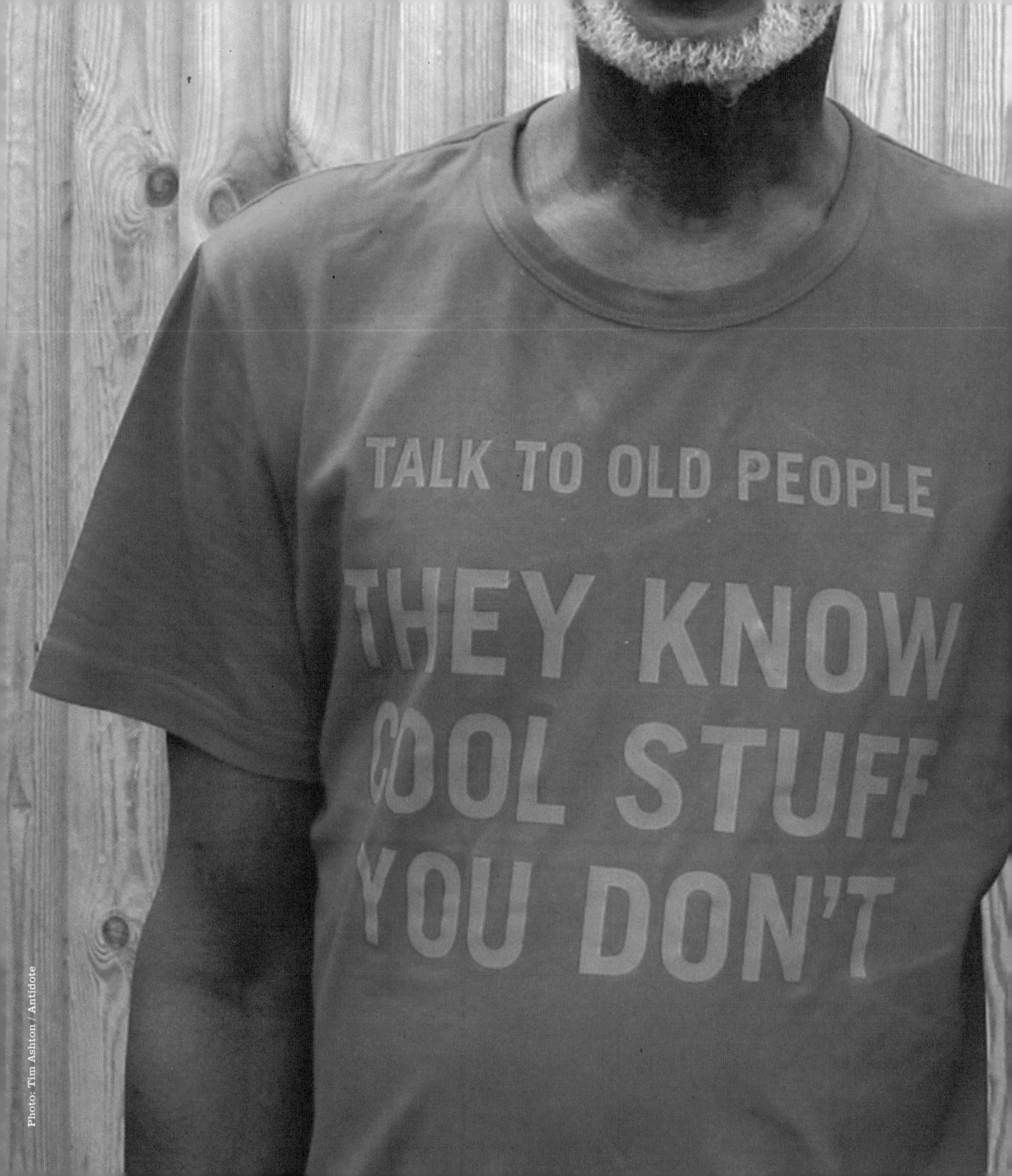

TALK TO YOUNG PEOPLE

THEY KNOW

COOL STUFF

YOU DON'T

After you've died, let your heart beat inside someone else's chest

Let your liver live, after you've passed on.

Even your eyes could give someone else a new look.

Nearly 4,000 Canadians are currently waiting for an organ transplant.
250 of them will die waiting. Over 90% of us support organ donation in
principle, but only 18% have joined their provincial organ donation register.

Maybe it's the hassle.
Maybe we've just never gotten around to it.
Maybe we think it's tempting fate.

Maybe.

The flip side is that registering as a donor might just change the fate of one of your fellow human beings by giving them the greatest gift of all, the gift of life.

To make sure your wishes are carried out, you need to do two things:

First, tell your next of kin about your wishes and ask them about theirs. Second, register on line where possible. You can find out how at www.givelife.ca

Make change

There's always loose change – and there are always charity tins.

It's a match made in heaven – like bacon and eggs, Gretzky and 99, or Bob and Doug.

If every time we ended up with a bit of change we looked for the nearest charity tin, the world would be a whole lot better off.

After all, 25 cents per person, per week, adds up to $390 million per year.

Rearrange your pictures.

Make a cocktail.

File.

Write a song.

Make faces in the mirror.

Jump in a lake.

Wear gold.

Revert to childhood.

Stay up all night.

Dance.

Turn left instead of right.

Streak.

Massage someone.

Dust.

Shave something off.

	Arabic	Mandarin	French	Bengali
Hello	Salaamu Alaikum (Peace Be Upon You)	Nee How	Bonjour	Assalam mu alaikum
Goodbye	Salaamu Alaikum (Peace Be Upon You)	Jie Jian	Au revoir	Khuda hafeez
Please	Min Fadluk	Ching	S'il vous plaît	Doya kore
Thank you	Shukran	Se Se	Merci	Doyno baad
Can I help?	Ma yumkin an as 'ad?	Wo leng bung oma?	Je peux vous aider?	Shajoy korte pari?
Would you like a cup of tea?	Sawfa anta/ani minal fanjan shai?	Ni yow bu yow yi bay cha?	Voulez-vous une tasse de thé?	Aponi ki cha pan korben?

uktitut

,

vvauvutit

ere is no word for
ease

ujannamiik

ajurunnaqpunga?

turiit?

Ikajurunnaqpunga?

Yes, you can help actually.

Just by learning a few words in a foreign
language, it's amazing how much genuine
warmth you can generate.

And in such a multicultural country as
Canada, you don't have to go far to meet
someone of a different culture.

It's a lot easier than you think.

For instance, in Arabic the word for "hello"
is the same as the word for "goodbye." Which
is a lovely sentiment, although it could make
telephone calls a bit confusing.

'...So the dog said...'

Make people laugh at you

Learn at least one good joke.

Laughing tones your stomach, lowers your blood pressure, and makes you healthier. It's scientifically proven.

Even the concentration of salivary immunoglobulin A is raised by laughing, and this guards our respiratory tract from infectious organisms.

But that in itself isn't very funny.

Unlike the two animals who meet each other in the forest. Asks the first animal: "What kind of creature are you?"

Answers the second animal: "I'm a wolfdog."

"What is a wolfdog?"

"Well, my daddy is a wolf and my mommy is a dog, so I'm half wolf, half dog, a wolfdog. And what kind of animal are you?"

"I'm a dragonfly."

"You're kidding..."

Make sure your investment fund has the same values as you

Unless you check that your money is ethically invested, chances are that you're supporting companies with poor human rights and environmental records.

Now, this is a complicated area, and even if you're just thinking about your investments, you deserve some kind of medal.

So, to make this as simple as possible – just ask your investment advisor one question: "Can you ensure that my investments don't harm the planet or hurt my fellow man?"

If we all did that, they would soon take notice.

But don't get caught up in a longer conversation, unless you're desperate for company.

As Woody Allen once said, anybody who wants to know the definition of eternity should try spending an evening talking to a life insurance salesman.

The most beautiful view of Toronto

All those offices with lights burning bright at night.

Are they really all full of people working late?

Or is it some crazy theory of aesthetics which says
that lighting an empty space is beautiful.

Ivory was considered beautiful once.

Fur was considered beautiful once.

Samuel Bratt, whose wife would not let him smoke, left her, in 1960, the sum of $660,000 on condition that she smoked five cigars a day.

Amateur footballer Sid Trickett's will in 1982 stipulated that his ashes be scattered at the Torrington Football Club goalmouth where he headed eight goals in 1948.

Dentist Philip Grundy, in 1974, left dental nurse Amelia White $362,000 on condition that she didn't go out with men or wear make-up or jewellery for five years.

In 1990 a lady left $200,000 to the King George Hospital for the "expansion, improvement and maintenance of its lavatories".

Ernest Digweed, in 1977, left $52,000 to Jesus provided it could be proved that his identity could be established.

Juan Potomachi, in 1955, left $60,000 to the Teatro Dramatico Theatre provided his skull could be used in Hamlet.

David Davis, in 1788, left his wife five shillings to "enable her to get drunk for the last time at my expense".

Hensley Nankivell requested, in 1987, that any relative wanting to benefit from his estate of $800,000 must first train as an airline pilot.

In 1926, Charles Vance Millar, a wealthy Toronto lawyer, bequeathed his estate to whichever woman gave birth to the most babies in the ten-year period following his death.

Think ahead

Make a will. Most bookstores
sell Make A Will packs for a
few bucks.

Or you can draw up a will
on-line (see Action 49).

For helpful advice on making
a will, visit www.cbc.ca/news/
background/wills/

And then you can make sure
that your goodies don't go to
the baddies.

We request...

the pleasure of your company tonight at the
kitchen table. Bring conversation.

Research has shown that children who have
meals with their families are much less likely to
suffer from anxiety or stress disorders.

George Bush Senior said that America needed
more families like the Waltons, and less like the
Simpsons.

A very bad idea, as it happens – after all, when
was the last time you laughed at the Waltons?

But if you notice, even the Simpsons like to eat
together.

AN INVITATION
DINNER

MEND IT RATHER THAN Replace IT

Glue it.

Screw it.

Tie it up.

Tape it down.

Darn it.

Oil it.

Sand it off.

Sew it back on.

Every time you repair something, you help the world's resources last a little bit longer.

Give away some great ideas

They dreamed up a scheme in Amsterdam a few years
ago, where white bicycles were provided free. And the
idea was that – after you finished your ride – you'd leave
the bike in the street for someone else to use free.

And if that isn't recycling, we don't know what is.

But unfortunately this idea flopped, because they failed
to take into account two things.

One, the fact that criminals exist.

And two, the fact that coloured paint exists.

But the idea was fantastically optimistic and deserved to
succeed.

A better version of this might be to ask people to
recycle their books. Give them to a charity shop, your
local library, or just leave one lying on a park bench –
although you might want to check the weather forecast

www.bloodservices.ca

THE MEDICAL
SIDE EFFECTS
OF GIVING BLOOD:

1. SLIGHT EUPHORIA

2. PUFFED UP CHEST

3. BROAD SMILE

The art of reverse haggling

Confuse the wonderful people who work in charity-run thrift stores. Pay them more than they bargained for.

Hungry?

One load of laundry in the dryer uses enough energy to make 250 pieces of toast.

We Are What We Do File Edit Window Help

Chuck it in the basement

Stick it behind the sofa...

Throw it out

Build an aquarium

Donate it to a school ⌘D

Mac Application: Noah Lieberman/N!yven

We Are What We Do

What we say about mobile phones in Action 13 applies equally to computers.

Except that computers are slightly heavier to carry down the street.

So, if you've got a computer you don't need anymore, contact any of the websites mentioned in Action 49, and they'll help you get it to someone who can make good use of it here or abroad.

Imagine the joy a twelve year old in the developing world would feel if they could play with the mightiest thing ever invented.

The thing you currently use to play 'Solitaire' and visit dating sites.

(Donate)

Get ready, get set, give

Next time you need to buy a friend a present, don't.
Make them one instead.

Gingerbread Men

3/4 cup	Brown sugar
1/2 cup	Butter softened
2	Eggs
1/4 cup	Molasses
3 1/4 cup	Flour
2 tsp	Ginger
1 1/2 tsp	Baking soda
1/2 tsp	Each : allspice, cinnamon, nutmeg and salt

Preparation

In a large bowl, beat sugar and butter until well blended.
Add eggs and molasses, and stir in remaining ingredients.
Cover and chill for 1 hour.

Roll out chilled dough on floured surface until 1/8 thick.
Cut into shapes.

Bake 10 minutes at 350°F/180°C. Cool on a rack. Makes
about 24 cookies.

Give away immediately.

0.7m

Save the world while brushing your teeth

Most people leave the tap running while brushing their teeth.

This wastes up to 9 litres of water a minute or 26,000 litres of water per family, per year.

This means your street alone could fill an Olympic sized swimming pool each year.

Which wastes huge amounts of water and is a bit stupid – it's like having the toilet flush the whole time you're on it.

So why not turn off the tap while you clean your teeth?

(We bet this is one of the actions you don't forget from this book. For some reason, it seems to strike a chord with everyone.)

A short cut to friendship

This action isn't just about mowing lawns. It's about finding simple ways to help people in your community. Collect a neighbour's mail while they're on vacation. Help someone by carrying their shopping.

They'll be grateful. You'll feel great.

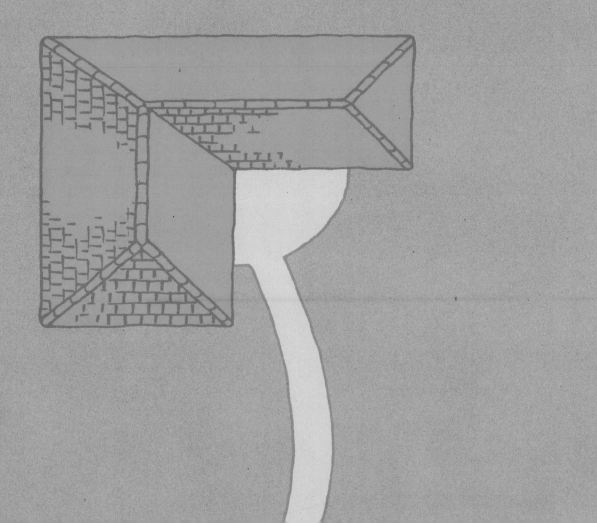

Illustration: Bob Shields.

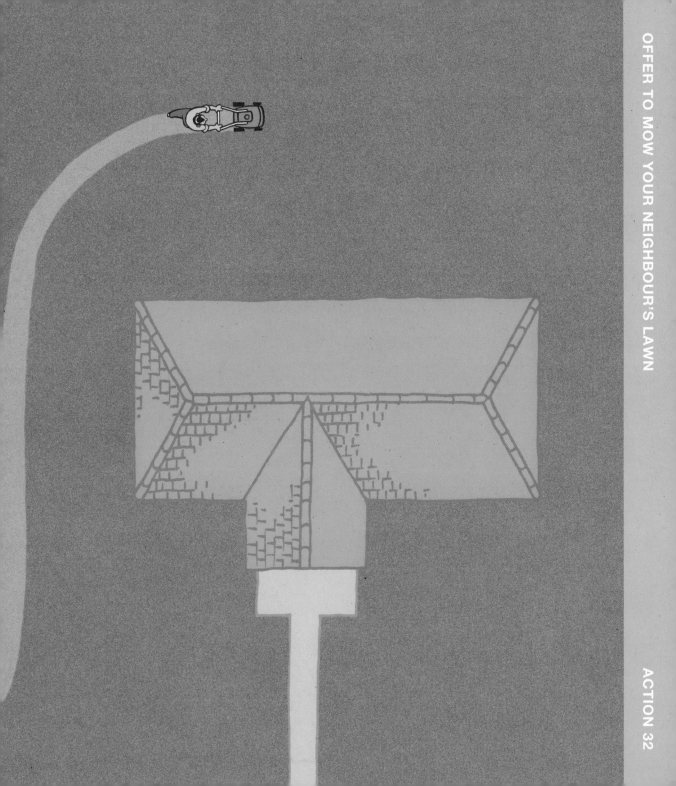

Give up your seat
to someone who needs it

Seeing people fall over is funny in movies.

In real life, they get hurt.

And unless you're in the subway, you'll get a better view standing anyway.

Not to mention it might result in an interesting conversation with someone of a different generation. (Action 14)

B.Y.O.M.

We use over eight billion disposable cups a year in Canada.

Where do they all come from? Is there some mad genius breeding them in underground bunkers?

I could have sworn I just saw two of them whispering to each other.

But why not put your coffee into a mug, not a diposable cup? It'll taste better, and you'll be doing your bit for the planet.

Nice to do. Nice to get. What's not to like about it?

ACTION 35
WRITE TO SOMEONE WHO INSPIRED YOU

Don't just do something, sit there

Right now, an estimated one million Canadians suffer from some form of depression.

Canadian Mental Health says that one in ten people will suffer from depression during their lifetime.

But there are lots of little things we can all do to make the world a less depressing place.

Like … just listening. It's a real art, actually – and not as easy as it sounds.

Listen to someone.

Don't make any comments, don't try to solve their problems.

Just listen.

After you

Beat road rage

Just about every driver has been the victim of road rage.

Here's an idea. When you're next at an intersection, let a car in ahead of you – but only if it's less cool than your own car.

If we all did that, the world would be a better place.

And if someone driving a K-car lets you in first, don't worry about it.

It's not personal.

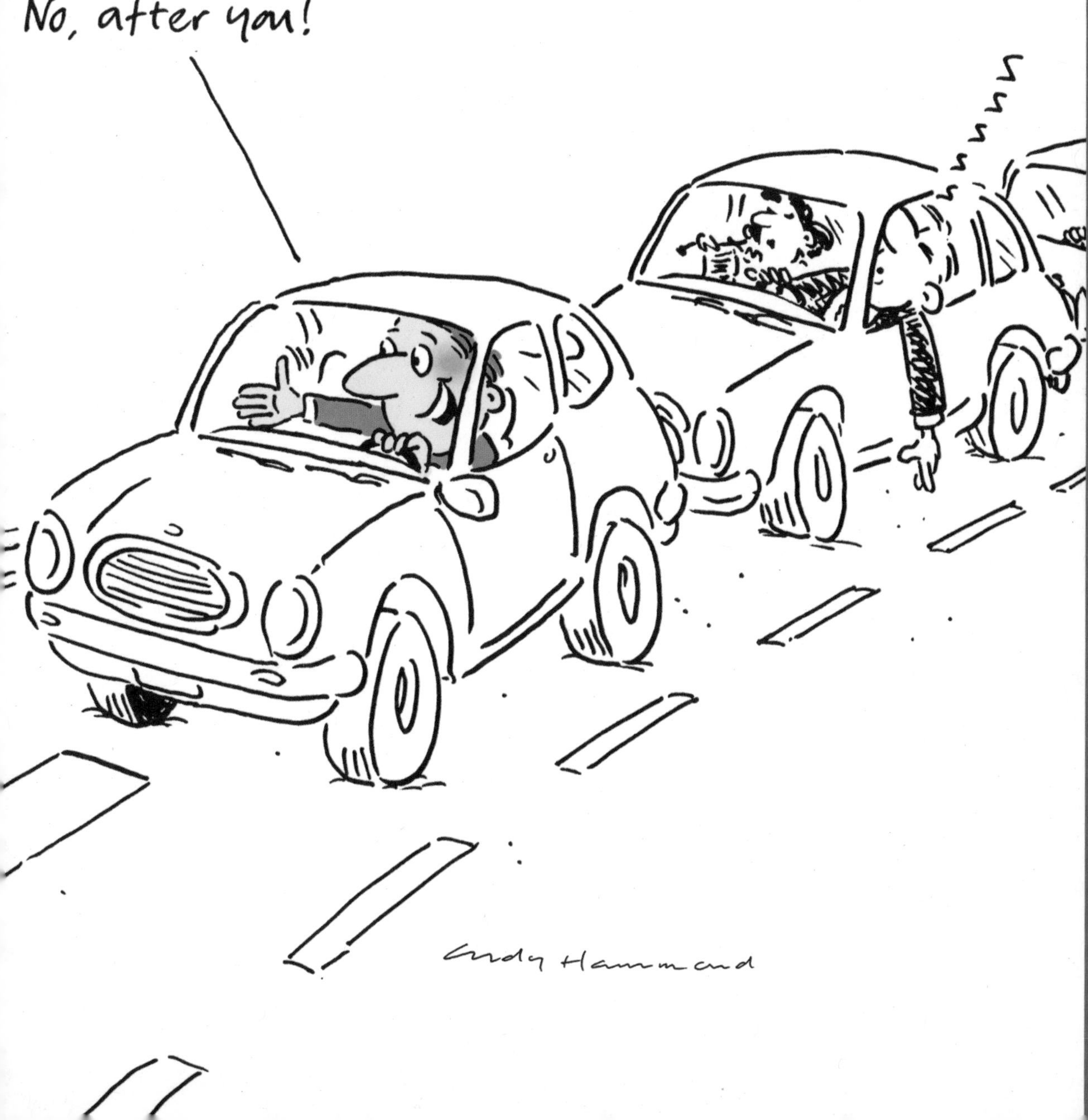
No, after you!

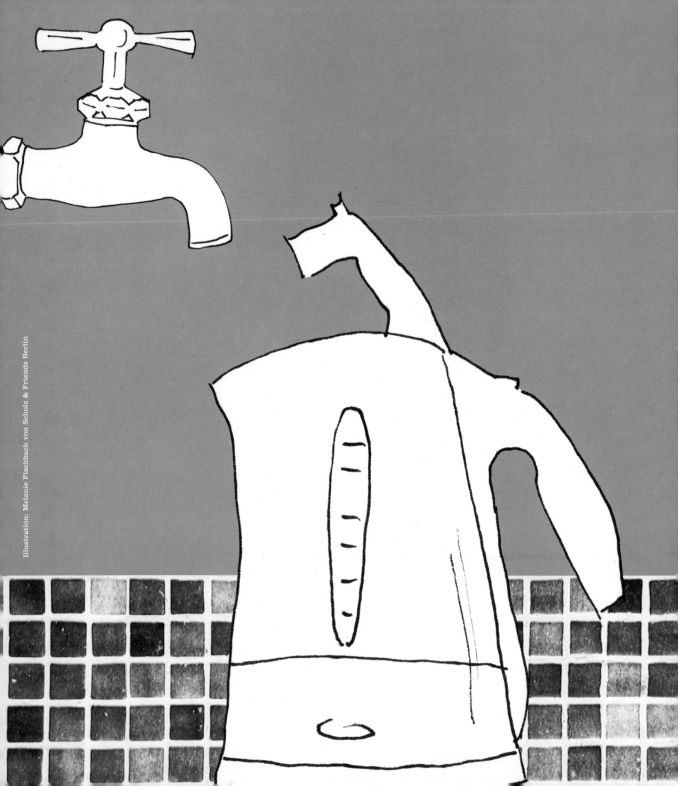

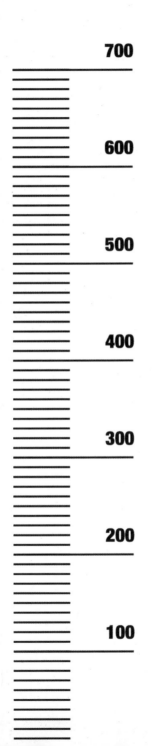

700

600

500

400

300

200

100

Only fill the kettle with the water you need

If everybody did this, we could save enough electricity to run all the street lighting in the whole country.

Apparently.

Whoever worked that statistic out should get out more. (Or maybe they can't, because the lights in their street don't work.)

We're

OPEN

Come on in and have a look around. How are you today?

We've got some of those cookies you said you liked. They're turning out to be quite a popular choice down the street. Oh, don't worry if you haven't got enough change on you, just give it to me next time you're in.

See you tomorrow.

We're

CLOSED

So sorry, hope you don't need anything too urgent.

The thing is, not enough of you have been coming to see us recently. We think it might have something to do with the big shop that's opened up down the road. We've loved being here but just can't afford to stay open any more.

See you.

aboriginalcanada.gc.ca amnesty.ca avalanche.ca barleyment.wort.ca blocquebecois.org
bookcrossing.com canadianbookclubs.com canadiancrimestoppers.org canadianstampnews.com
chess.ca clubsmartcar.ca conservative.ca consumer.ca coopscanada.coop corkscrewnet.com
davidsuzuki.org earthrangers.ca enablelink.org farmfolkcityfolk.ca fastlife.ca glassartcanada.ca
goforgreen.ca greenparty.ca greenpeace.ca greenteacher.com indexingsociety.ca killerwhale.org
laughteryoga.ca liberal.ca librarianactivist.org lung.ca mineralogicalassociation.ca ndp.ca
plentyoffish.com recycle.net scasoccerschool.com sciencewriters.ca skatecanada.ca slowfood.ca
songwriters.ca spca.com swimming.ca traincollectors.org trooper.ca walks.ca wearewhatwedo.ca
whiteribbon.ca wienerdogs.com womennet.ca workplace.ca youcan.ca zoetrope.com

Stamps, trains, corkscrews, speed
skating or speed dating; whatever it
is you are into, these days, you can be
part of the community without even
leaving home.

Joining in is as simple as logging on.

Don't be idle

When you're stopped for more than 10 seconds, it pays to turn off the engine.

That's about as long as it takes to say:

Engine idling from vehicles contributes particulates and other pollutants to the atmosphere affecting the health of people and the environment. Pollutants from automobiles contribute to acid rain, ozone formation, and global climate change.

Although you may prefer the more conventional:

One Mississippi,

Two Mississippi,

Three Mississippi ...

Every year thousands of pairs of glasses could be flown to developing countries

Many of us have old pairs of glasses lying around unused. Yet 200 million people around the world need glasses every year. People who can't see properly can't do their jobs, and kids who can't see properly can't learn at school.

So show some foresight. Find the nearest place to donate at www.clerc.ca

A TV that's on standby is still using a lot of electricity

And a VCR on standby uses almost as much electricity as one playing a tape.

The same applies to DVD players, computers, printers, stereos etc.

Switching that little 'standby' light from green to red doesn't actually do you, or the planet, much good.

It's still costing you money and wasting energy.

Unplug it.

A man walked by a candy wrapper on this sidewalk yesterday. He frowned and said 'tsk, tsk'.

Today he walked by another wrapper, picked it up and put it in the garbage.

He felt much better.

Lend a hand,
help clean up Canada

Next time you pass a piece of litter on the
street, why not pick it up?

You won't get the cooties. We promise.

Talk to strangers
Start next door

Give your phone number
to 5 people on your street.

Why not?

They could help you, you
could help them, you could
make new friends.

My name is: _____

I'm your neighbour

My phone number is: _____

Please call if I can help

My name is: _____

I'm your neighbour

My phone number is: _____

Please call if I can help

My name is: _____

I'm your neighbour

My phone number is: _____

Please call if I can help

My name is: _____

I'm your neighbour

My phone number is: _____

Please call if I can help

My name is: _____

I'm your neighbour

My phone number is: _____

Please call if I can help

we are what we do©

we are what we do©

we are what we do©

we are what we do©

we are what we do©

Use of every paper

It's estimated that over 170 million trees are cut down every year for the paper that's used in Canadian offices.

So much for the so-called paperless office which everyone was writing all-staff memos about a few years back.

But if we used both sides of the sheet – for instance by pressing the button that says "use both sides of the paper" on the photocopier – we could halve this.

Let's create a culture in which we make it socially unacceptable to use only one side of paper.

both

sides

of

piece

Isn't this a little bit self-serving, an advertisement for our book in the middle of our book?

But this isn't about making money, it's about making change.

So, after you've bought your copy, buy another. And then give it to the person you think needs it most.

P.S. Don't forget to reuse the wrapping.

What would you like one million people to do?

One man or woman can change the way we act every day.
One such man was Martin Luther King.

Send us your ideas for what you'd like one
million people to do, and we'll make them part
of the We Are What We Do movement.

suggestions@wearewhatwedo.ca

The simple actions in this book are just a beginning.
Discover more from these websites and go further. We are what we do.

01	LEARN MOUTH TO MOUTH	www.sja.ca www.redcross.ca/firstaid
02	DECLINE PLASTIC BAGS WHENEVER POSSIBLE	www.bringyourownbag.ca www.reusablebags.com
03	SPEND TIME WITH A CHILD	www.childrencanada.com www.scholastic.ca/kids www.raffinews.com
04	TAKE PUBLIC TRANSIT WHEN YOU CAN	www.carpooltool.com www.gotransit.com
05	HUG SOMEONE	www.thishugsforyou.com
06	PLANT SOMETHING	www.tree-planting.com www.gardenline.usask.ca
07	INSTALL AT LEAST ONE ENERGY-SAVING LIGHT BULB	www.miltonhydro.com/lighting.html www.oee.nrcan.gc.ca
08	GET FITTER, FEEL BETTER	www.tips-for-boomers.com/walking.html www.saferoutestoschool.ca www.studentsonice.com
09	BUY FAIRLY TRADED PRODUCTS	www.transfair.ca www.fairtradeconcepts.com
10	TURN YOUR THERMOSTAT DOWN BY 1°	www.utilitieskingston.com/info/esavings.html www.energyalternatives.ca/conservation.asp
11	SMILE AND SMILE BACK	www.worldsmile.org www.smileycollector.com
12	IF IT SAYS 40 – DO 40	www.pedsafe.com www.safety-council.org/info/traffic/speed
13	RECYCLE YOUR MOBILE PHONE	www.pitch-in.ca www.charitablerecycling.ca
14	SPEND TIME WITH SOMEONE FROM A DIFFERENT GENERATION	www.carp.ca www.youth.gc.ca
15	REGISTER ONLINE AS AN ORGAN DONOR	www.givelife.ca
16	GIVE YOUR CHANGE TO CHARITY	www.canadian-charities.com www.canadahelps.org
17	TRY WATCHING LESS TV	www.tv-b-gone.com www.whitedot.org
18	LEARN TO BE FRIENDLY IN ANOTHER LANGUAGE	www.200words-a-day.com www.purelanguage.ca www.itk.ca
19	LEARN ONE GOOD JOKE	www.freejokes.ca
20	FIND OUT HOW YOUR MONEY IS INVESTED	www.socialinvestment.ca www.ethicalfunds.com
21	TURN OFF UNNECESSARY LIGHTS	www.bchydro.com/business www.energy.gov.on.ca

22	USE YOUR WILL TO GOOD EFFECT	www.ethicalwill.com
		www.lawdepot.com
23	HAVE MORE MEALS TOGETHER	www.parenthood.com/recipe.html
		www.mealsmatter.org
24	BE RESOURCEFUL	www.reuses.com
25	RECYCLE YOUR BOOKS	www.cla.ca
26	GIVE BLOOD	www.bloodservices.ca
27	PAY MORE WHEN YOU BUY AT CHARITY-RUN THRIFT SHOPS	www.thriftstores.ca
28	HANG YOUR WASHING OUT TO DRY	www.electricitychoices.org
		www.fortisbc.com
29	RECYCLE YOUR COMPUTER	www.era.ca
		www.worldcomputerexchange.org
30	BAKE SOMETHING FOR A FRIEND	www.joyofbaking.com
31	TURN OFF THE TAP WHILST BRUSHING YOUR TEETH	www.eartheasy.com/live_water_saving.htm
32	OFFER TO MOW YOUR NEIGHBOUR'S LAWN	www.learndirect.co.uk
33	OFFER UP YOUR SEAT	www.toronto.ca/ttc/coupler/0705/25_billion.htm
34	USE A MUG NOT A DISPOSABLE CUP	www.saltspringcoffee.com/merchandise.html
35	WRITE TO SOMEONE WHO INSPIRED YOU	www.allaccolades.com
		www.mandela-children.ca
36	TAKE TIME TO LISTEN	www.eqi.org/listen
		www.suicideinfo.ca
37	LET AT LEAST ONE CAR IN ON EVERY JOURNEY	www.caa.ca
38	DON'T OVERFILL YOUR KETTLE	www.prohardware.ca/tener.htm
39	SHOP LOCALLY	www.farmfolkcityfolk.ca
		www.nsfarmersmarkets.ca
40	JOIN SOMETHING	www.wearewhatwedo.ca
41	TURN YOUR ENGINE OFF	www.treehugger.com/files/2005/09/treehugger_home.php
42	RECYCLE YOUR GLASSES	www.clerc.ca
43	UNPLUG ELECTRONICS WHEN NOT IN USE	www.standby.lbl.gov
		www.pioneerthinking.com/electricitybills.html
44	PICK UP LITTER	www.pitch-in.ca
45	GIVE YOUR PHONE NUMBER TO 5 PEOPLE IN YOUR STREET	www.neighbourhoodwatchregistry.com
		www.blockwatch.com
46	USE BOTH SIDES OF EVERY PIECE OF PAPER	www.recycling101.ca/officePaper.html
47	BUY A COPY OF THIS BOOK FOR A FRIEND	www.wearewhatwedo.ca
48	SEND US AN ACTION	www.wearewhatwedo.ca
49	LEARN MORE, DO MORE	www.wearewhatwedo.ca
		www.davidsuzuki.org
		www.greenlearning.ca
50	DO SOMETHING FOR NOTHING	www.volunteer.ca

We Are What We Do does not receive money from any websites
mentioned in this book and is not responsible for their content.

Many people have contributed to the creation of this book.

We would especially like to thank the following:

IN THE UK:

Illustration Ltd for working with their illustrators to create the images.

Getty Images for collaboration on the photography.

The Book Service (part of the Random House Group) for providing storage and distribution.

Innocence and **ArthurSteenAdamson** for the creation of the We Are What We Do brand.

Wieden + Kennedy for creative support throughout the development of We Are What We Do.

Cathay Pacific for providing travel facilities.

Antidote
Allen & Overy LLP
Apna Ghar
Brunswick Group
Business in the Community
Channel 4
Community Links
Good Business
Interbrand
Lyndales Solicitors
Royal Mail
Short Books
Three Blind Mice
TimeBank
Time Life
White Door

IN AUSTRALIA:

We Are What We Do is forever grateful to Pilotlight Australia who it worked with to produce and publish **Change the World for Ten Bucks**. This book would not have been possible without Pilotlight Australia and the generous support of the following organisations:

Hardie Grant Publishing
Whybin\TBWA and Amy Smith
Freehills
Deloitte
Pacific Brands
Macmillan Distribution Services

IN DEUTSCHLAND:

All den wundervollen Menschen des **Pendo Verlags** für die Unterstützung bei der Zusammenstellung, dem Vertrieb und der Vermarktung dieses Buches.

SCHOLZ & FRIENDS Berlin für ihre kreative Leistung, Inspiration und Geduld bei der Umwandlung des englischen Buches in sein deutsches Gegenstück.

Nicki Kennedy von der **Intercontinental Literary Agency** für ihre Unterstützung bei den ersten entscheidenden Schritten in Deutschland.

GoodBrand&Co
FH Mainz
Gepa
Miami Ad School

IN CANADA:

The Canadian publication of **Change the World for Ten Bucks** would not have been possible without the generous support of the following organizations:

New Society Publishers for believing in the project and donating their time and resources.

Noah Lieberman of **N'lyven Design** for hanging out every Tuesday and making it look fantastic.

Smith Communications for passionate public relations support.

Toumbi (Steve Heynen) and **Martin Russocki** for illustrations.

We Are What We Do in the UK, Australia and Germany.

and...

to everyone not listed here, oops! Thank you for helping to change the world without acknowledgment!

INDIVIDUALS

Alan Reinhart
Andrew Heintzman
Angie Renick-Hayes
Ania Russocki
Bill Yetman
Brenda Woods
Coulter Wright
Derek Fry
Diane McIntosh
Debbie Edney
Dena Lieberman
Elliot Smith
Francisco Garcia Klänhammer
Jake Hayes
James Beresford
James Loeppky
Jeremy Thompson
Jim Maclean
Joel Kalia
Joel Soloman
John Alton
Julie and Matt Fry
Kevin and Jo O'Callaghan
Kristin Finstad
Marcus and Amy Garvey
Maria Long
Mark Brownlie
Martin Russocki
Martin Rydlo
Michelle Beeson
Mike Serbinis
Natasha, Maia and Seth Edney
Pamela Loeppky
Phil Solman
Rachel & James Edney
Raya Lieberman
Scott Beffort
Steffanie Rundle
Suzie Gignac
Tania Freedman
Tatiana Petron
Tilion Lieberman

ORGANIZATIONS

Allen & Overy LLP
Campbell's Soup
Community Cave
David Suzuki Foundation
Earth Rangers
Friesens Corporation
Green Teacher
Inuit Tapirit Kanatami
Kate Walker & Co
Omnipresent Productions
Otter Books
Passion for Action
Retail Council of Canada
Students on Ice Expeditions
Tridel

Booksellers across Canada for making sure **Change the World For Ten Bucks** is within easy reach.

and...

we are what we do ☺

NEW SOCIETY PUBLISHERS

ENVIRONMENTAL BENEFITS STATEMENT

New Society Publishers and We Are What We Do have chosen to produce this book on recycled paper made with 100% post consumer waste, processed chlorine free, and old growth free.

For every 5,000 books printed, New Society Publishers saves the following resources:[1]

19	Trees
1,740	Pounds of Solid Waste
1,914	Gallons of Water
2,497	Kilowatt Hours of Electricity
3,163	Pounds of Greenhouse Gases
14	Pounds of HAPs, VOCs, and AOX Combined
5	Cubic Yards of Landfill Space

[1]Environmental benefits are calculated based on research done by the Environmental Defense Fund and other members of the Paper Task Force who study the environmental impacts of the paper industry.